Snapshots AND Stories

Snapshots and Stories

Increasing Awareness of God's Faithfulness Through the Practice of Journaling

Amy Meyer

Introduction

It was early on Christmas morning and we had waited as long as we could. When we got the okay from Mom and Dad, I led the way down the stairs in birth order from youngest to oldest: me, Scott, Liz, then Steve. The excitement grew as we turned the corner and saw the tree decorated for the first time and all the presents piled beneath it. We tore into our presents. One of the gifts was a calendar for each of us, complete with fun stickers to mark special occasions.

It seemed like a simple gift at the time, but as I think back, that was when my practice of writing began. I was seven. This practice started with filling in the little calendar squares with details about my day; the day's events, where I went and who I met. I then moved to keeping a diary, full of my thoughts and feelings, which became more of a prayer journal over time. For most of my life, I have practiced remembering by writing.

We tend to be forgetful.

"Write it down so you don't forget." How often have you heard those words? And it is true.

We don't just forget what to buy at the grocery store or to pick up the dry cleaning

or send a birthday card, we also forget important memories and events from our past. Think about the memories that stick. It is often because those are the stories that are told over and over again. We are also prone to forget the attributes of God and His powerful presence in our lives. One of the reasons the Jewish faith has so many festivals to celebrate is to remember what God has done.

"We will not hide them from their children, but tell to the coming generation the glorious deeds of the Lord, and his might, and the wonders that he has done. He established a testimony in Jacob and appointed a law in Israel, which he commanded our fathers to teach to their children, that the next generation might know them, the children yet unborn, and arise and tell them to their children, so that they should set their hope in God and not forget the works of God."

(Psalm 78:4-7 English Standard Version)

The Psalm goes on to recount how the children of Israel passed through the Red Sea on dry ground and were delivered from their enemies. And how God provided them guidance in the desert with the cloud in the daytime and the pillar of fire at night. And how he fed them manna from heaven and gave them water from a rock.

Then verse 35 says, "They remembered that God was their rock, the Most High God their redeemer."

They remembered and in the next few verses there is a but, because they quickly forgot. The pattern is repeated throughout scripture, remembering and forgetting.

This book provides a way for you to practice remembering by writing. Whether you love to journal or have never tried journaling before, the prompts at the end of each story will give you a starting place. You will begin to establish a pattern of writing about your story and how God has shown up in your life. Each chapter is a snapshot of a story from my life, in no particular order. Many of the details have been left out, and I have focused on the lesson I learned about myself or my God. God's Word is the greatest story ever written, and I have selected a verse from His Word to go with each story.

I am passionate about recording what is happening in my daily life, as well as pouring out my heart to my heavenly Father in written prayers. It has provided me not only the benefit of being able to recall what has happened, but I am also reminded of how faithful God has been. I am given courage and confidence, knowing he will be with me into the future.

You will benefit from taking time to reflect on your own story, remembering what God has taught you and then you will be more ready to share your story with someone else. God in his faithfulness and love has pursued, provided, and protected you. There are others who will benefit from hearing what you have to say about our awesome, powerful God. Often it is easier to know what to say once we have written it down.

"DON'T PUT OFF UNTIL TOMORROW WHAT YOU CAN DO TODAY."

— Benjamin Frank lin

Give journaling a try today. As you read the stories in this book, the temptation will be to read them and move on. I challenge you to consider *your* story. Take time to be intentional and set aside 10 minutes to write down your initial thoughts, feelings, or memories in the space provided. Don't worry about grammar or if it makes sense. Just write. Begin the practice of reflecting on how God has worked in your life, remembering the stories and writing them down.

Remembering what God has done for you will prompt you to give him praise and thanks. The more you praise and thank God, the more you will realize how able and powerful and good He is, and the more you will trust him moving forward.

The Final Thoughts section has some generic journal starter questions listed and tips for journaling. Write about your day, where you went, who you met. Write about your thoughts and feelings. Write out your prayers to God. Write what you are thankful for. Just start writing, a little every day, and watch what happens.

Everyone has a story and I thank you for taking the time to read some of mine. Go grab a pen and enjoy the journey.

Acknowledgments

Thank you to...

Lynn and Anneke for asking me when I would write my book and encouraging me to go for it,

my mom for modeling a journaling lifestyle, and my dad for loving me so well,

Mom and Dad Meyer for giving me grace from the first day they met me,

my husband Jeff who wrote his book first and showed me it was possible. Thank you for reminding me I could do it and encouraging me all along the way, I love you,

my daughters Kyla, Kacie, Abbey and Alli for cheering me on and being such important people in my story,

my sister Liz for being my biggest fan, my brothers Steve and Scott for always believing in me,

Jackie for mentoring me and investing in me all those years ago,

Kirsten who cared enough to read it before anyone else, and pushing me across the finish line,

Kylie who showed a genuine interest and gave me helpful feedback,

Beth for the careful editing,

and to God for remembering me and loving me enough to send your Son Jesus to die for me, for rising again and living everyday with me. Thank you that one day I will spend eternity with you sharing stories around your throne and singing praises forevermore.

Contents

CHAPTER 1

Words That Stick

We were eating lunch in our third grade classroom and I decided, while our teacher Mrs. Weber was out of the room, it would be fun to do an experiment. How many times would it take for a carton of milk to be thrown up to the ceiling before it would break? A few of my classmates joined me in this experiment. Mrs. Weber came back into the classroom and we were caught in mid-throw! Thankfully it was before any of the cartons broke open! Mrs. Weber pulled me aside and said these words, "Amy, you are a leader. You will have a lot of chances to lead people and they will follow you. You can lead them to do good things. Or, you can lead them to do bad things." Well, her words stuck with me. And I believed them. At age 9, I believed I was a leader, an influencer. I have thought back to that day several times throughout my life. I used to think it was a weighty load to put on a young child. Yet I believe God used Mrs. Weber in my life in a very positive way. I don't remember getting in trouble (I should have, what a naughty thing to do). What I remember was being told, "you are a leader", and having those words instill great confidence in me.

Words are powerful. We can encourage and build others up or we can tear them down, all with words. The childhood rhyme "Sticks and stones may break my bones, but words can never hurt me" is a straight-up lie. Words can hurt, and they can do a lot of lasting damage. Perhaps you are living with words that were spoken to you when you were a child or teenager and you still can't shake them. Those messages do not need to define you, especially if they are lies. It takes hard work and with some increased intentionality, you can be free of those words and replace them with the truth.

To whom can you speak words of blessing and affirmation? What a gift you can give to young boys and girls. Recognize what their natural gifts are and tell them.

I am thankful for Mrs. Weber and how she handled the silly milk carton incident. Truth be told, we are all leaders. You are a leader. You influence others every day. Other people are paying attention to how you handle situations in your life. Lead well.

"Do not let any unwholesome talk come out of your mouths, but only what is helpful for building others up according to their needs, that it may benefit those who listen."

(Ephesians 4:29 New International Version)

Your Turn

What messages or words are sticking to you that you need to be free of? Try the exercise of writing the lie in one column and on the opposite side write the truth. (Turn to scripture and look at what God says about who you are) What messages or words have stuck with you that you are thankful for? Who can you encourage? What will you say?

_____

_____

_____

_____

_____

_____

_____

_____

_____

_____

_____

_____

_____

_____

CHAPTER 2

God Knows Best

I was certain I would get the summer job. I was finishing up my freshman year at the University of Missouri and was told about an awesome summer job at a Christian sports camp, Kanakuk. I was good at sports. I played basketball, field hockey and ran track in high school. I loved working with kids, and I loved Jesus, so no problem. It was going to be for  only one month out of the summer which was perfect since I was hoping to connect with friends back home. It was close to home, which seemed comfortable and easy to manage. I interviewed — and did NOT get the job. I was so disappointed. I didn't understand. And to make matters worse, a friend who also interviewed DID get the job. So now what? My brother encouraged me to apply for a summer project through the ministry of Campus Crusade for Christ. The only project that still had openings was in Wildwood, NJ, and it would be for the entire summer. I applied and was accepted. What had I gotten myself into? I didn't want to be gone all summer long, and how was I going to get all the way out to New Jersey? It all seemed so out of my comfort zone and difficult to manage.

All the pieces fell into place to make my journey out to Wildwood. Halfway through the summer, the staff leaves, and all of the college students take on different leadership roles. My assignment was to help with the prayer ministry. We would spend time praying for each other and for those all around the world who are persecuted for their faith. We also took time to pray for those who are far from God, that they would come to an understanding of just how much God loves them. I was stretched out of my comfort zone, especially with the experiential learning we did and the evangelism outreach events on the beach. I was challenged and my faith grew. I met amazing people from all over the country. I have such fond memories of that summer, and it didn't take me long to realize I was exactly where God needed me to be the summer of 1984. Camp Kanakuk would have been great, but I already knew I was good at sports and working with kids and liked being not too far from home. God wanted to teach me NEW things. I sure am thankful He is in charge!

"Trust in the Lord with all your heart and lean not on your own understanding; in all your ways submit to him, and he will make your paths straight."

(Proverbs 3:5-6 New International Version)

Your Turn

When in your life did something not go how you really wanted it to go? How did you process the disappointment? How did God use it for good? What if anything are you thankful for from that time?

_____

_____

_____

_____

_____

_____

_____

_____

_____

_____

_____

_____

_____

_____

_____

_____

_____

_____

CHAPTER 3

He Sees Me

While flying to Fort Collins, CO, to speak at a women's retreat, I was reading a book called "Jesus Life Coach" by Laurie Beth Jones. It was the chapter, "With Jesus as your life coach you will be seen." The author wrote that as a teenager, when she first began to fall in love with Jesus, she requested a little personal ritual between the two of them. She asked that whenever he is thinking of her, he would send her a ladybug. At the end of the chapter, she asked these questions:

1. Do you have a little love ritual with God?

2. If not, why not?

3. If so, what is it?

4. Do you believe that God sees you right where you are?

5. Do you believe that you are worthy of a special ritual? (You are.)*

---

* page 54
2004 Nashville, TN Thomas Nelson, Inc

I thought about it for a moment and wrote down "Dolphin" and "Hummingbird". I put the book and my journal away and didn't give it too much more thought. I was picked up at the airport and taken to the home where I would be staying for the weekend. My gracious hostess showed me to the bedroom, and I put my things away. To the right of the bed there was a glass dolphin statue. "Oh,  wow!", I thought. Then, I turned to leave the room and next to the door on the wall hung a picture of — you guessed it — a hummingbird! I just started laughing to myself. "Thanks, Lord, for the sweet reminder, You see me. You love me. You are with me." Since then, God has had so much fun using special sightings of dolphins and hummingbirds to remind me of his deep love for me. Like the time I went to Ethiopia, and my shower curtain at the hotel was covered with dolphins! Or on vacation in Florida, walking along the beach and getting to watch for several minutes as dolphins were playing in the ocean right in front of me. While struggling to put a leash on a dog who I was being paid to take on a walk, I looked up and there was a metal hummingbird hanging by the window. Or at the airport gift shop looking at little glass sculptures and the dolphin and hummingbird were hanging side by side. God loves to delight his children. He loves to remind us of his presence.

In the Old Testament book of Genesis, there is a story about a woman named Hagar. She was a servant of Sarai and Abram. Sarai took matters into her own hands when she and her husband were having trouble conceiving a child. Sarai told her husband to sleep with Hagar and, sure enough, Hagar got pregnant. Sarai was then filled with jealousy and rage and sent her away. While

Hagar was running away, God stopped her and asked where she was going. He then told her to return. And this is what she said:

> *"She gave this name to the Lord who spoke to*
> *her: "You are the God who sees me," for she said,*
> *"I have now seen the One who sees me." That*
> *is why the well was called Beer Lahai Roi; it*
> *is still there, between Kadesh and Bered."*

(Genesis 16:13-14 New International Version)

Beer Lahai Roi means *well of the Living One who sees me.*

Yes, indeed, our God sees us, knows us, loves us and is with us.

Your Turn

What would you pick for your personal ritual with God and why?

_____

_____

_____

_____

_____

_____

_____

_____

_____

_____

_____

_____

_____

_____

_____

_____

_____

_____

CHAPTER 4

Personal Mission Statement

I was first challenged to have a personal mission statement in 1990 while attending the Pastoral Leadership Institute and going through a process called Leading From Within. I came up with something, but it felt generic, like it could be anyone's mission statement. Several years later, I attended a worship and the arts conference with our team from church. While we were on a break, I sat by a fountain and reviewed my workshop notes. And it came to me that I want to *be filled to overflowing*. I pictured a three-tiered fountain. As I fill up from God's Word and with His love, I can then overflow to others. That year I was intentional about asking myself some questions to see if I was on track. How are you doing, Amy, at filling up with God's love and His Word? Who are you spending time with that is benefitting from that love pouring out on them? Or are you keeping what you have received to yourself? I then searched Scripture to find a verse that would help to remind me what I wanted to be about. I found this:

"The Lord will guide you always;
he will satisfy your needs in a sun-scorched land
and will strengthen your frame.
You will be like a well-watered garden,
like a spring whose waters never fail."

Isaiah 58:11 (NIV)

In 2016, I went through a life design course, The Younique Experience, and we were challenged to boil down our life's call to only 2 words. You could also have a sentence that describes your mission statement, but they really wanted you to land on two words. It was a difficult and rewarding process to consider all the options and word combinations. After a great deal of work, here is what I came up with:

Restoring Buoyancy

I live to remind the overwhelmed how to return to the source of joy.

I am thankful for the different people who have led me to reflect and process and discover what God's call is on my life. God has a purpose for each one of us. It is no mistake that you are here. You are unique. You are the only you there is. Discover what your purpose is and live it out with great confidence!

"You have made known to me the paths of life;
you will fill me with joy in your presence."

(Acts 2:28 New International Version)

Your Turn

Do you have a life verse from the Bible? What is it? If you have never picked out a life verse, try picking one today. Have you thought about what your personal mission statement would be? Take some time and consider it. What might your two words be?

CHAPTER 5

Surprise

Tired from the long journey back home from Addis Ababa, Ethiopia, I waited for my luggage so I could clear customs at Dulles International Airport in Washington D.C. and then make my final connecting flight home to Madison, WI. I made it to my gate and noticed there were several others standing at the counter who had been on my flight. Our next flight was overbooked. I had my boarding pass and went to the counter and was told, "You weren't here in time so you might have to forfeit your seat." What? That made no sense to me. I was at the gate in plenty of time. I have a seat on the plane reserved for me that I have paid for. I waited. There was a lot of confusion and then finally I was told I could board. I sat in my seat, put my backpack under the seat in front of me and breathed a heavy sigh of relief. One step closer to being home. I looked up and the man that had been at the gate was now standing in the front of the plane and the next thing I know they were calling my name and escorting me OFF OF THE PLANE! What? "I'm sorry ma'am, your seat has been given to someone else. You need to come with me." Wait, what? Are you kidding me? There were three others who also had not gotten on the flight. We all compared stories and couldn't believe this was happening.

I was tired, angry, annoyed, tired, disappointed, tired, frustrated — and did I mention I was tired? Sure enough, the tears started, and I couldn't get them to stop. One of the ladies who was also now having to adjust to different travel plans came over and comforted me. "Hi," she said, "I'm Ellen". I tried to compose myself and managed to say, between sniffs, "I'm Amy". She was traveling with a team of people who had just been on a medical missions trip in Ethiopia. She said, "You can wait with us. We are going to get something to eat. Do you want to come with us?" What a surprise gift this new friend was! I suddenly realized I wasn't alone, and she could help me figure out how to get home a different way. We waited in the long line together and were issued a generous check from the airline. We exchanged stories from our time in Ethiopia and even prayed together. The time passed quickly with my new friend. We added one another as Facebook friends, and it has been such a joy to keep in touch. I did finally make it home after waiting on standby on three different flights. I made it as far as Chicago, and my sweet husband drove and picked me up to take me the rest of the way home.

> *"We can make our plans, but the*
> *Lord determines our steps."*

(Proverbs 16:9 New Living Translation)

Your Turn

Think about a time when you had an unexpected turn of events. What was the surprise gift included? When have you been the surprise gift to someone else?

_____

_____

_____

_____

_____

_____

_____

_____

_____

_____

_____

_____

_____

_____

CHAPTER 6

Teach Us To Number Our Days

It was a sweltering day, August 2007, in Dallas, TX. My husband was attending a board meeting, and I came along. I had free time and went for a stroll to see if I could find a spot to be still for a bit and sit with Jesus. I had my journal, a pen and my Bible, and I set off to try to find some shade. What I found was a perfect spot by a little stream. There was a hollowed-out section on the side of the stream for me to sit. I dipped my toes in the cool water and listened to the sound of the babbling brook. A large, red dragonfly came by and entertained me for a while. I was actually cool by the stream in the shade, even though it was 100 degrees. I was overwhelmed with the thought that God had been waiting for me to find this spot on this day. He knew I would be there. I must have sat there for a couple of hours, reading my Bible, journaling about how thankful I was for this special time alone with Jesus. I felt my empty tank filling up. My soul was being hydrated.

I went back to my hotel room, and my phone rang. On the other end was our oldest daughter crying so hard I could barely understand her. Once she took a couple deep breaths, she was able to tell me the news she had just received. The girl who was supposed to be her college roommate, Alicia, was killed in a car accident. I couldn't believe it. Kyla did not know her, she had only talked with her a few times, planning out who was bringing what to the dorm room. Kyla and I talked a little more on the phone, and then we had to hang up. Oh, how my heart broke for Alicia's family.

I marched back outside into the heat, this time with a basketball in my hand. I pounded the ball into the pavement over and over, and I cried. It could easily have been my daughter driving home from work and crashing her vehicle. We would soon be saying goodbye to our daughter and moving her into a dorm. This dear family didn't even get to say goodbye, and their daughter moved into heaven. I was so very thankful for the morning I had just experienced by the babbling brook. Because of how full I was with the love and peace that comes from God's Word and His presence I was able to handle the news in the moment that Kyla shared with me so much better. I could be strong for her and point her to Jesus.

Kyla and I decided to attend the funeral. I will never forget how long Alicia's mom held onto Kyla. She said, "Everyone here represents my daughter's past. But you represent the future that she would have had." She told Kyla to do her very best at college and to enjoy every moment. Life is precious, and we do not know the number of days we have. I was reminded again to make the most of each day and keep short accounts with those I love.

"Teach us to number our days that we
may gain a heart of wisdom."

(Psalm 90:12 New International Version)

Your Turn

Consider a time in your life when you had extra rest or time with Jesus that prepared you for something that came later. When was that? Describe it. Where can you go and sit in a special space with Jesus? When will you make time in your schedule to meet with him? He is waiting for you.

_____

_____

_____

_____

_____

_____

_____

_____

_____

_____

_____

_____

_____

_____

_____

_____

CHAPTER 7

Grace

It was November of 1988, and I was in Keystone, CO, attending a Christian Singles Conference with some of my college girl-friends. We would snow ski during the day and have inspirational, challenging presentations and discussions in the evening. I will never forget the evening that I left the session bawling. The small group discussion question was simple, "What do you think will be your biggest challenge in the new year, 1989?" Why did that question send me bawling out of the session and into the cool mountain air? Well, I had a secret: I was pregnant.

I went outside, by myself, and fell to my knees. I cried out to my Heavenly Father, "Please help me. I can't do this alone. I'm scared. I'm sorry. Forgive me and help me figure this out." That night, I told my friends the news, and they gave me love, grace, hope and a shoulder to cry on. I knew I had to go home and tell my parents, siblings and co-workers, and I was dreading those conversations. I disappointed a lot of people. I had a lot of shame and guilt and rejection to work through. With each conversation, I was shown grace upon grace and experienced forgiveness in ways I never had before. I was determined that I would have this little baby, and we would be OK.

July 13 came, and I was blessed with the gift of a tiny baby girl. Yes, 1989 was full of challenge — and also the most wonderful year, as I became a mother. On February 9, 1990, I went on a blind date with a man named Jeff Meyer, a seminary student. He was singing in a talent show with four other guys called, The Master's Voice, an a cappella group. A woman I worked with, Sandi, arranged the

date. I didn't want to go. My sister talked me into it and offered to babysit. I'm so glad I went! On July 21, 1990, I married Jeff Meyer, and he adopted my sweet little girl. Grace upon grace, blessing upon blessing. In August, we moved to Florida, where he had his year of internship as a pastor. God took us over 1,000 miles away from everything we knew so we could work on being a family of three. We had a lot of adjustments to make and a lot to learn. (Playing at the beach and Disney World helped make it a little easier!) Every time I think about this part of my story or share it with someone, I am amazed at the goodness and faithfulness of God and His extravagant grace.

*"For from his fullness we have all re-
ceived, grace upon grace."*

(John 1:16 English Standard Version)

Your Turn

Where have you experienced forgiveness and grace in your story? What does it look or feel like to allow the grace of God to wash away your guilt and shame? Who in your life needs forgiveness and grace extended to them?

_____

_____

_____

_____

_____

_____

_____

_____

_____

_____

_____

_____

_____

_____

_____

_____

CHAPTER 8

Dear Jesus Thou Art Everything to Me

What fun to be at our best man's wedding just a year after ours! Mark and Theresa got married June 30, 1991, and Jeff was the best man. So we flew from Florida to Chicago, then drove to Iowa, for the wonderful event. I remember dancing at the reception and suddenly doubling over in pain. Unsure what was happening, I sat down and took it easy. Sunday came. We went to church, and the pain was so great, I needed help to walk up the stairs. We flew back home to Orlando, and Monday was a pretty normal day and the pain had lessened. Tuesday morning came, the pain came back and I was extremely weak. I called my mom, because that's what daughters do. She was very serious on the other end of the phone and said, "Find someone to watch Kyla, and have Jeffrey drive you to the ER now!" I did what she said. And, lying there in the ER, we learned two things. 1. I was pregnant. 2. Something was wrong. Before I knew it, I was being whisked away to surgery.

As I was wheeled down the hall, I had an extraordinary sense of peace, and this song in my head. "Dear Jesus thou art everything to me, and everything I own I give to Thee. My life, my all, but most of all, Dear Lord, I give myself to Thee." It is a camp song that I had recently heard sung while we were celebrating at the wedding. I knew in that moment, no matter what, that Jesus was with me and would take care of me.

It turns out that I had an ectopic pregnancy, and my fallopian tube had ruptured. The weakness I felt was due to significant internal bleeding. While I recovered, I had to come to grips with being so thankful I was alive, and so full of sadness that we lost our baby.

Some of what we learned during that time has been invaluable.

- *You can pray for someone over the phone.* Thanks to my brother Scott, who was living in California at the time. He could not be with us, and instead of saying, "I'll be praying for you" he prayed for us over the phone. It is something we have done for others as well as writing out the prayer in an email or text.

- *Sometimes people say things that are hurtful even though they are trying to help.* Often people don't know what to say and they don't mean to be insensitive. Perhaps it is better to just say, "I am so sorry."

- *It is important to go through the grieving process, even if you never met the child that you lost.*

- *God is close to the brokenhearted, and He will comfort you.*

- *God provides loving people at just the right time.* We are close friends to this day with the family that cared for Kyla during my time in the hospital. Thanks, Bruce and Rox!

- *God can do the impossible and work miracles.* I was told it would be difficult to conceive and have any more children. God blessed us with three more daughters!

> *"Though the fig tree does not bud, and there are no grapes on the vines, though the olive crop fails and the fields produce no food, though there are no sheep in the pen and no cattle in the stalls, yet I will rejoice in the Lord, I will be joyful in God my Savior."*

(Habakkuk 3:17-18 New International Version)

Your Turn

Think back to a difficult event or situation that happened in your life, what lessons did God teach you? List the lessons and give Him thanks. Practice the, YET I will rejoice in the Lord, from the above Bible verse.

CHAPTER 9

Rule Follower? Or Rule Breaker?

Are you a "rule follower" or a "rule breaker"? That is a fun icebreaker question to ask to a small group of people. Most people don't have any trouble answering it. They know right away which one they are. My answer is, "I follow the rules  when I think it is a good rule. If I don't think it is a good rule, or not worthy of following, then for sure, I am a "rule breaker." I am not necessarily proud of this. I mean, it does fall into the category of disobedience and well, sin. Nevertheless, I have many examples.

Small things, like the do not enter sign at the high school parking lot. I justify this in my head that I need to get to a certain door and pick up my child, and no one is coming so it is safe. *Yes, I know, I should go around and follow the rule.* Or, the no parking sign outside the grocery store. I think to myself, "I'll just be a few seconds while I return the movie to the Redbox." *Yes, I know that is justifying my behavior and it is still wrong, it says no parking.*

My husband particularly likes to tell this story as a prime example of me thinking rules don't apply to me. This one almost got me in a lot of trouble. We were in Hong Kong as part of a Pastoral Leadership Institute team, training pastors and their wives. My daughter Kyla and I were exploring the grounds of the training center and found a beautiful creek with some large rocks. It looked like a perfect place to take some photos. So, we opened the gate, went inside and took some pictures. We were interrupted, however, by a Chinese guard — with a gun — who asked us to come back on the other side of the fence. Then he pointed to the sign that clearly stated, "Do Not Go Beyond This Point". I would love to tell you the sign was in Chinese so we couldn't read it, but it was in Chinese AND English. No excuses. I simply didn't think the rule applied to me, because I wasn't going to do anything wrong, just capture a great photo.

Thankfully, the guard was understanding, and we did not get thrown into any kind of jail. The photos did turn out nicely. I have tried to change since then. I think twice before breaking a rule. I used to think it was just kind of humorous that I don't follow the rules. However, the more I reflect on thinking rules are not for me, the more I realize it is a matter of sin and disobedience. God has asked us to obey his rules. They are called commandments, and it is not ok for me to pick which ones I want to follow and which ones I don't.

*"Today the Lord your God has commanded
you to obey all these decrees and regulations. So
be careful to obey them wholeheartedly."*

(Deuteronomy 26:16 New Living Translation)

Your Turn

How do your rule following or rule breaking tendencies affect your relationships or other areas of your life? Think of a time you either followed the rules or broke them. What was the outcome? In what ways do you justify your behavior?

CHAPTER 10

Where Are You Looking?

A few years ago, I read *The Art of Racing in the Rain* by Garth Stein. It is a book written from the perspective of a golden retriever. His owner is a race car driver. I have zero interest in car racing, but my youngest daughter loves dogs, and she knew that her oldest sister, an English teacher, used this book in the classroom. Because it came so highly recommended to me by two of my favorite people, I read it. It did not disappoint.

There was a repeated theme in the book, a phrase that was used several times. This race car driver was so good at racing in the rain because of where he set his gaze. Here is the quote: "The car goes where the eyes go." The other way he said it: "That which we manifest is before us."

It matters where we set our eyes. It matters where we look.

Hebrews 12:2 (New Living Translation) says: "We do this by keeping our eyes on Jesus, the champion who initiates and perfects our faith. Because of the joy awaiting him, he endured the cross, disregarding its shame. Now he is seated in the place of honor beside God's throne."

Keeping our eyes fixed on Jesus makes a difference. It is kind of like what happens when you put a magnifying glass over something. It gets bigger. When we keep our eyes on the Lord, we magnify HIM and not ourselves and our problems. As Psalm 34:3 (English Standard Version) says, "Oh magnify the Lord with me, and let us exalt his name together!" Keeping our eyes on Jesus helps us keep our focus where it belongs. It helps change our perspective.

There is an awesome example of this in the Old Testament in 2 Chronicles, Chapter 20, about a man named Jehoshaphat. He was about to be involved in a big battle and he was afraid. He gathered with many people and they prayed together, and I love what he says in verse 12: "For we have no power to face this vast army that is attacking us. We do not know what to do, but our eyes are on you." (New International Version) Isn't that awesome? He was not sure what to do, but he knew where to look. It is a matter of being intentional about where we look.

It certainly gets difficult to look up and fix our eyes on Jesus, in the midst of deep grief and sadness and uncertainty.

I attended the funeral for a 21-year-old young man who was killed in a car crash. The church was packed with loving family, friends and community. There was so much hurt and pain. "What does the family do tomorrow?", I wondered, the day after they buried their son. How do they get up and go on?

The next day came, and I turned to my daily journal, working through the Psalms, and the truth was there again: "I lift up my eyes to the hills. From where does my help come? My help comes from the LORD, who made heaven and earth." (Psalm 121:1-2 English Standard Version) It was the Psalm that was read at our wedding. I have read it many times, but this time I was reminded that this dear family would do just that. They will lift up their eyes to the one who made the heavens and the earth, the one who died for their son, the one who conquered death and the grave, the one who claimed their son in the waters of baptism. They will fix their eyes on Jesus, the one who said, "I am the resurrection and the life. Whoever believes in me, though he die, yet shall he live." (John 11:25 English Standard Version) And I will do the same.

> *"I lift up my eyes to the hills. From where*
> *does my help come? My help comes from the*
> *Lord who made heaven and earth."*
>
> (Psalm 121:1-2 English Standard Version)

Your Turn

What are your eyes fixed on? What are you magnifying? What could you do to remind yourself to fix your eyes on Jesus? What would your day look like if your eyes were fixed on Jesus?

_____

_____

_____

_____

_____

_____

_____

_____

_____

_____

_____

_____

_____

_____

_____

CHAPTER 11

Go Ahead, Smile!

Growing up in St. Louis, MO, we went to the zoo a lot. It was free! Sometimes we would go and just see a few of the animals and go back home. More often than not, while we were at the zoo, my mom would find a small child who was crying and had gotten lost from their mom or dad. She would patiently and lovingly calm down the child and find a zoo official to help.

I was always amazed at how comfortable my mom was at jumping in to help. There was also no such thing as stranger danger to my mom. I think of the quote, "strangers are just friends waiting to happen" (Rod McKuen). That is what my mom modeled for me. I thought everyone struck up conversations with people in the elevator, the line at the grocery store, or in the neighborhood. Saying "Hi" being interested in the other person, showing genuine care for those in need, is how my mom lived her life. I'm happy to say, it rubbed off on me.

Fast forward to just a few years ago at a mall in Madison, WI, where my daughters and I were shopping. Sure enough there was a little girl crying and scared and lost from her parents. My daughters and I tried to calm her down and see if we could locate her family. Thankfully, I had my daughter Kacie with me who spoke more Spanish than I do, and she was able to talk with the little girl's abuela (grandma) and they were reunited. First thing I said, "My mom would be proud!"

I think one of the most important things we can teach our children and grandchildren is to treat each person you meet with all the love and kindness with which you would like to be treated. Each person is worth full value. Each person is made in the image of God. We have no idea how far a simple act of kindness will go.

I realized this first hand when we left our first congregation in West Des Moines, IA, and went to serve at First Immanuel in Cedarburg, WI. As part of our farewell, people wrote us letters to say thank you. I received a letter from a woman thanking me for greeting her with a smile when she first came to our church. She went on to say she was very uneasy about coming to church and would not have stayed around except that I smiled at her and asked if she wanted someone to sit with her.

Quite honestly, I don't remember doing that. It wasn't hard. I was just being friendly. I had no idea the impact it made. She ended the letter by saying, "I am sad that you are leaving but I know there are more doors for you to stand in and smile so someone else will feel welcome."

"Do to others as you would have them do to you."

(Luke 6:31 New International Version)

Your Turn

Who from your childhood had an impact on how you interact with others now? What lessons did you learn, positive or negative, from that relationship? What are you modeling for those who are watching you? How are you doing at showing love and kindness to others?

_____

_____

_____

_____

_____

_____

_____

_____

_____

_____

_____

_____

_____

_____

_____

CHAPTER 12

Draw Near With Confidence

I have grown in my appreciation, understanding and practice of prayer over the years. It was modeled for me as a young child: We always prayed before we ate and gave thanks before we could get down from the table. I was blessed to grow up in a Christian family and learned very early on to pray the Lord's Prayer and Now I Lay Me Down To Sleep at bedtime. (Sometimes that ended in a giggle session with my siblings and parents). I learned that I could just talk to Jesus like I would talk to a friend, about anything, anytime, anywhere. My mom modeled writing out prayers to God as she would journal. What an amazing gift to look back and see how faithful God has been to answer those prayers! Sometimes God says no, sometimes he says not yet, sometimes he says yes, and sometimes he says yes and here's more! What a privilege it is to know that we can, as the writer to the Hebrews said, draw near with confidence to our Lord in prayer. "Let us then with confidence draw near to the throne of grace, that we may receive mercy and find grace to help in time of need." Hebrews 4:16

When my children were in elementary school, I was invited to participate in a Moms In Prayer group. We would gather weekly and pray for our children, their teachers and the schools. One of the things I loved about the group was we always began with praising God for who He is. God is able, God is all-powerful, God is good, God is with us, God is our Provider, God is our Rock, God is all-knowing, God is our deliverer, God is faithful… What this did was remind us how awesome our God is, and it took the focus off ourselves and our problems. We would take time to silently confess what we were sorry for and then take time to say "thank you" for how God was working in our children's lives. Then we would take a verse from Scripture, put each child's name into the verse and cover that child in prayer. It was powerful to soak them in the promises of God. What a gift it was to hear other moms pray for my children. Check out www.momsinprayer.org for more information.

I have also enjoyed going on prayer walks. I walk around the neighborhood, letting what I see inform how I pray. For example, you walk past a cemetery and you can pray that God would comfort those who are grieving. Pray for the teachers and the safety of the students when you pass a school. When you see toys in the driveway of a home, pray for the health of the children that they will grow up knowing they are loved by Jesus and for the strength of the marriage of their parents. There are so many needs and so many things to pray about. I have noticed that as I walk through my neighborhood and pray for those I know and those I don't, God begins to give me His heart and His eyes for the people. I long for my neighbors to know that God loves them and sent His son Jesus to die and rise for them so they can have eternal life forever with him.

"O Lord, hear me as I pray; pay attention to my groaning. Listen to my cry for help, my King and my God, for I pray to no one but you. Listen to my voice in the morning, Lord. Each morning I bring my requests to you and wait expectantly."

(Psalm 5:1-3 New Living Translation)

Your Turn

Who can you pray for right now? What scripture verse could you pick to place their name in and write out a prayer for them?

_____

_____

_____

_____

_____

_____

_____

_____

_____

_____

_____

_____

_____

_____

_____

_____

_____

_____

_____

CHAPTER 13

A New Song

It was the fall of my junior year in college, 1985. To this day, I am not exactly sure what happened to begin my slow, steady downward spiral. Slowly, I started to lose my joy. I was burdened by not knowing what I wanted to do with my degree, speech communication, and how I would even get a job. Most of the people with my major were going into sales, and I wanted nothing to do with that. I even thought about dropping out of school and being a flight attendant.

I had gained weight and felt self-conscious about my appearance. I was living in a sorority and was non-stop comparing myself to everyone else, and I didn't measure up: not pretty enough, not thin enough, not smart enough. And I didn't have a boyfriend. Pretty soon, I found it difficult to get out of bed and go to class. The easiest of tasks were almost impossible for me, like picking out something to wear or get past, "Hi, how are you?" in a conversation. All I wanted to do was sleep.

I remember one of the most difficult things was having to stand up in front of the class and deliver a speech. I had nothing to say. I had zero motivation to research a topic and inform or persuade anyone of anything. It was scary to feel so different than I had felt for most of my life. Bubbly, outgoing, happy, positive …and none of those words described me in those days, weeks and months.

I called home and tried to explain it to my mom and cried out for help. I went home one weekend, and my dad helped me write a speech using his knowledge of the heating and air conditioning world. My mom, who has always been my prayer warrior, began to plead with God to put a song back in my heart.

I talked with trusted friends, went to counseling for a while and slowly God began to answer my mom's prayer. Slowly, I began to feel like my old self and was able to want to sing again. King David wrote a lot of Psalms when he was struggling with doubt, discouragement and despair. I am so thankful he modeled pouring out his heart and real feelings to the Lord. Psalm 40 has become very special to me.

I have great compassion for those who struggle with depression or anxiety. I understand there are many whose struggle goes on for years or even a lifetime. My heart goes out to them, and I pray they are able to have moments of hope and joy.

"I waited patiently for the Lord; he turned to me and heard my cry.
He lifted me out of the slimy pit, out of the mud and mire; he set
my feet on a rock and gave me a firm place to stand. He put a new
song in my mouth, a hymn of praise to our God. Many will see and fear
the Lord and put their trust in him."

(Psalm 40:1-3 New International Version)

Your Turn

When have you experienced a time of discouragement or depression? During these times, what steps can you take toward healing? What verses in scripture do you hold onto? What help are you seeking? Who could you talk and pray with?

_____

_____

_____

_____

_____

_____

_____

_____

_____

_____

_____

_____

_____

_____

_____

_____

_____

CHAPTER 14

Not My Plan

I was on my way to Addis Ababa, Ethiopia, and this time I was traveling alone. I would meet up with the rest of the team in Frankfurt, Germany and fly the rest of the way with them. I arrived and went to our meeting place. No one I recognized was there, but there was a big crowd of people. I started overhearing bits of conversations, "No flights are leaving", "The airlines are all on strike." I finally found the rest of my team and, sure enough, a 24-hour strike was happening, and we could not fly on to Ethiopia as planned. I was very thankful I was not alone at this point and the three of us could make a plan together. We got on a train and made our way to a hotel and found a place to eat. I let my family know back home how the travel plans had changed. The next morning, I received a phone call from a man who lives in Frankfurt. He is a pastor, and he and his wife are friends with my father-in-law. My father-in-law had reached out to let them know of our circumstance. Before we knew it, Pastor Bob and Rita Flohrs were picking us up, and we spent the day together touring the Rhein River area by Rudesheim. We went to some wonderful places and ate delicious food and had a beer or two. We were able to get our flight booked and what came next was an awesome surprise — and the definition of grace. All three of us on our team were upgraded to first class! I have never flown first class, WOW! We did nothing to deserve this upgrade. It was a gift given freely, just like grace!

Besides the hassle of missing our scheduled flight, one of the reasons it was so disappointing was we also missed a special added trip to Hawassa before our training began in Addis. We were all looking forward to getting to the southern part of the country and seeing our brother in Christ, Hailu. What I didn't know then that I know now and am so thankful for, is I would return two years later to Addis in 2016 with our youngest daughter Alli, and she and I would get to go and experience Hawassa together. The memories we have from that portion of our trip are amazing. We were able to be in Hailu and Zelalem's home and meet their beautiful family. We were able to have coffee and share hospitality with another family in their home and experience more of the countryside. I am so very thankful my first attempt to go to that city was canceled so Alli and I could go together.

This story is another example of how God has a plan, and He is sovereign and always good and knows what is best for us. I need to trust Him. He is trustworthy!

"As the heavens are higher than the earth,
so are my ways higher than your ways and
my thoughts than your thoughts."

(Isaiah 55:9 New International Version)

Your Turn

Think of a time in your life when your plans did not turn out like you thought they should. What happened in your life as a direct result? What lessons did you learn as you look back? Are there any unfinished stories, that you are eagerly awaiting to learn how God might use them?

CHAPTER 15

The Lost Is Found

When my husband and I celebrated our 25th wedding anniversary, we had the opportunity to stay at our friend's home in Coeur d'Alene, Idaho. Neither of us had ever been there before, and it was absolutely beautiful.

On one of the days we hopped in our rental car and drove to Glacier National Park to explore more of God's amazing creation. We were not disappointed. Every time we came around another corner, we were in awe of the majestic mountains and turquoise water rushing past in the streams or waterfalls. We decided to stop and hike down to an area with some cool rocks and take some pictures. There are a lot of marked trails in Glacier, we however went off trail and meandered our way through the woods. We made it down the hill and got some awesome shots.

As we hiked our way back up to the road to get back in the car, Jeff asked me for the keys. I then realized I did not have the keys! He thought I was kidding, but unfortunately, I was not. Immediately I started praying. We would need a miracle to find those keys. We did not have another set for the rental car, and I had no idea where I lost them. Remember, we were not on any marked trail. We retraced our steps through the woods, and we found them!! I started saying out loud with great passion, "Thank you, Jesus! Thank you, Jesus!"

I have to say, I really didn't think we would find them. When I prayed for help, truly knowing we needed a miracle, I don't think I believed God would really care about our lost car keys. I was so relieved and grateful, especially because it was my fault!

Here are some things I learned:

1. If you don't have a safe pocket for your keys, give them to someone who does.

2. Don't tuck your keys in your yoga pants and think they will stay there.

3. Miracles happen. God cares about the little details of our life.

4. My husband was very loving and patient in that mini-crisis.

5. Just think how much rejoicing there is in heaven when a lost person is found!

"Just so, I tell you, there will be more joy in heaven over one sinner who repents than over ninety-nine righteous persons who need no repentance. Or what woman, having ten silver coins, if she loses one coin, does not light a lamp and sweep the house and seek diligently until she finds it? And when she has found it, she calls together her friends and neighbors, saying, 'Rejoice with me, for I have found the coin that I had lost.' Just so, I tell you, there is joy before the angels of God over one sinner who repents."

(Luke 15:7-10 English Standard Version)

Your Turn

Think about a time you lost something. Describe the situation below. What was the outcome? Do you know people in your life (friends, family or neighbors) that are far from God? Write out a prayer for them, ask God to pursue them so there will be much rejoicing by the angels in heaven when they are found.

CHAPTER 16

Eucharisteo 1000

Back in 2000, my doctor said, "Some ovarian cysts just go away on their own, this one unfortunately is not going away, and we need to do surgery." Those were not the words that I wanted to hear.

She was hopeful that she could remove the softball-sized cyst and that there would be no further trouble. I had the surgery, we got the amazing word "benign" (non-cancerous) delivered to us, and I went home.

As I was reflecting in my journal about the experience, I wrote out a prayer of thanks to God for the good news. I remember saying to friends and family how thankful I was when I shared the news with them. And then, it hit me: Would I still be thankful if the news was different? If she would have come out of the surgery with the dreaded word "malignant" (cancerous) would I have been able to still be thankful? Was I only thankful when things went well? Would I only be thankful if things turned out like I wanted them to?

What do we do with the verse in 1 Thessalonians 5:18 — "Be thankful in all circumstances, for this is God's will for you who belong to Christ Jesus"? (1 Thessalonians 5:18 New Living Translation) It says ALL circumstances. What if the circumstance is one that you don't want to be in? We can still give thanks to God because God is always good, and we are always loved.

The act of writing down what you are thankful for is practicing a thankful life. Practicing a thankful life became very real to me some years later, when I received a special gift for my birthday.

A friend gave me a book, *One Thousand Gifts A Dare to Live Fully Right Where You Are* by Ann Voskamp. She also gave me a small journal. The author was challenged by a dare one of her friends gave her. "Could I write a list of one thousand things I love? To name one thousand blessings—one thousand gifts -?" pg.45

She took the challenge and wrote a wonderful book about the relationship between grace, thankfulness and joy. The reason my friend included a journal with the book was so I could take the challenge as well. Because I love to journal, I accepted the challenge. I did not worry about writing in this journal every day, and I didn't worry about the number of things I wrote down. Some days I wrote one thing, some days I wrote five.

Here is what I began to notice: I became much more aware of what was taking place in each one of my days. I began to look for what I could be grateful for. And because I was writing down so many different things I was thankful for, I was very specific.

I took note of very small things; nothing was insignificant. I wasn't just thankful, I was expressing my thanks to God. It made a positive difference in my attitude. There was something powerful about writing these notes of gratitude down in the journal, and what a wonderful record to have to go back and look at.

Consider this quote from Ann Voskamp in *One Thousand Gifts*: "Is the height of my *chara* (joy) dependent on the depths of my *eucharisteo* (thanks)?" Page 33 Let that sink in. There is an amazing connection between joy and thanks.

I reached 1,000 and have now started a new journal. There is always more to be thankful for, more gifts of joy to unwrap. "God gives gifts and I give thanks and I unwrap the gift given: joy." Page 57 Now you know why my name on Instagram is Eucharisteo1000.

> *"I will give thanks to you, Lord, with all my heart; I will tell of all your wonderful deeds."*

(Psalm 9:1 New International Version)

Your Turn

What are you thankful for today? What have you been able to give thanks for that didn't seem "good" at first? What would it take to start the habit of writing down what you want to thank God for? Why not start right now? Can you list 10 things you are thankful for from the past week?

_____

_____

_____

_____

_____

_____

_____

_____

_____

_____

_____

_____

_____

_____

CHAPTER 17

My Dad

Heads would turn and people would stop us and ask, "What is THAT?"

Growing up, we had the privilege of owning a ski boat. And because my Dad was a mechanical engineer by trade and could design and make pretty much anything, he rigged up a way to keep all the ski ropes organized on a pulley system. We could ski up to eight skiers at a time! We made quite a scene on the lake when we would have that many skiers up at once!

My dad was always inventing things and making them happen. Like the "camper box". He made a large sheet metal box where Mom could pack all the non-perishable food items we would need for going on a two-week camping trip. The first model was so heavy, he had to lift it into the boat with a crane! The second model was improved as each section came out, making it not as heavy. It became a portable kitchen for mom at the campsite, complete with a surface to do dishes.

He also designed a ski pole where there were two experienced water skiers on the ends and the person learning how to ski in the middle. We taught countless numbers of people to ski using that pole.

I had one of the best science fair projects in elementary school as my dad helped me turn my Fisher Price dollhouse into a model showing how solar panels work. When I was in high school, I played basketball, and he made a contraption to help me keep track of how many free throws, layups and jump shots I made while practicing at our hoop in the backyard.

His creativity, know-how and desire to bless others has continued. He surprised us while my husband and I were gone for a week in South Korea by refinishing the dining room table I was given from my grandfather. He made a giant dollhouse for our oldest daughter when she was eight, complete with lights that worked. He made our daughters four-post canopy beds for their dolls, and a horse stable for Kacie.
And when our daughter Kyla asked him to help her build a playhouse for her children, he said yes and supervised the project. He was 84 at the time!

I love that my dad used the skills and gifts that God gave him to bless others. These were just a small sample of the projects he completed. Not only did he create and fix and build, he passed on his deep, abiding faith in His Lord and Savior Jesus to his children and grandchildren and great-grandchildren. He modeled grace and forgiveness and love. I am forever grateful for my dad.

"His master replied, 'Well done, good and faithful
servant! You have been faithful with a few things;
I will put you in charge of many things."

(Matthew 25:21 New International Version)

Your Turn

Consider your relationship with your father, whatever that relationship might be. What lessons did you learn? What memories or stories come to mind? Remember, no matter what type of earthly Father you had, your Heavenly Father loves you perfectly and always has your best in mind and promises to never leave you or forsake you.

CHAPTER 18

Make His Word Stick

Not long ago I was having an extremely difficult time. In the midst of my struggle, I began paging through my Bible, looking at familiar passages I had highlighted. I found myself in Lamentations 3:20-23.

> *"My soul is downcast within me. Yet this I call to mind and therefore I have hope. Because of the Lord's great love we are not consumed, for his compassions never fail. They are new every morning; great is your faithfulness."*

(Lamentations 3:20-23 New International Version)

Not only was this already highlighted in my Bible, but verses 22 and 23 have been put to music, in a song I have sung hundreds of times.

On this particular day, however, something jumped off the page at me as if I'd never read it before.

"YET THIS I CALL TO MIND AND THEREFORE I HAVE HOPE."

I stopped and took a big deep breath and asked myself this question. What do I need to call to mind so I can have hope?

In this passage, it is the Lord's great love and his compassion that never fails. It is the amazing gift that his mercies are new each and every morning. They never wear out or get old. Because God is so faithful, I can depend on God and I can trust him. I can trust him even when things don't make any sense and in times of uncertainty and change.

I took another big deep breath and stopped to say "thank you" to God. I thanked him for his word. No matter how many times we may read a passage or hear a familiar story from the Bible, it can be new and remind us in a new way of what we need to know. That is because His word is alive and active. (Hebrews 4:12) The Holy Spirit gets our attention with what we need to know and be reminded of. It is so important to memorize scripture and hide God's word in our heart so we can call it to mind and have hope.

"And now, dear brothers and sisters, one final thing.
Fix your thoughts on what is true, and honorable,
and right and pure, and lovely, and admirable. Think
about things that are excellent and worthy of praise.
Keep putting into practice all you learned and received
from me—everything you heard from me and saw
me doing. Then the God of peace will be with you."

(Philippians 4:8-9 New Living Translation)

Your Turn

What do you need to call to mind today? When has knowing scripture by heart helped you in your life? What verse do you want to be intentional about memorizing? Tips for memorizing scripture: Say the verse out loud and repeat it several times. Write out the verses on a 3x5 card and carry it with you. Put the verse to a tune and sing it. Write it out several times.

CHAPTER 19

Full Value

The room was full of pastors' wives, and we were attending a retreat as part of our training with the Pastoral Leadership Institute. Jackie Oesch was sharing a devotional message with us. She was talking about just a few verses from the Gospel of Luke, a story that was unfamiliar to me. It was about the bent-over woman.

> *"On a Sabbath Jesus was teaching in one of the syna-gogues, and a woman was there who had been crippled by a spirit for eighteen years. She was bent over and could not straighten up at all. When Jesus saw her, he called her forward and said to her, "Woman, you are set free from your infirmity." Then he put his hands on her, and immediately she straightened up and praised God."*

(Luke 13:10-13 New International Version)

After we discussed for a while about the different things we could learn from this passage, Jackie went on to talk about what happened as she was preparing to give us this message.

Often on her morning walks, she would come across a penny on the road. She would find some that were slightly scratched up and others were almost unrecognizable as they had been driven over so many times. She got to thinking about the value of those pennies: Was the scratched penny worth any less than a shiny new penny?

The answer is no. No matter how scratched up the penny is, she could take it to the bank, and it would still be worth full value. That is when she had an idea: She wanted to have scratched up and tarnished pennies made into keychains to give to each one of us so we would remember that we are worth full value in the eyes of Jesus no matter what has happened in our lives that has bent us over.

She went to the bank and told the teller what she wanted to do. And the woman's eyes filled with tears and said, "You were sent here to tell me that story. I have been told all my life that I don't matter and I'm not worth anything. But what you are saying is that I do have value."

Well, the story does not stop there. We each received those key chains and then Jackie had many, many more made. I have had the privilege of giving that same message to women in China, Ethiopia and Kenya, Colorado, Ohio and Wisconsin and Indiana. I still carry the keychain today.

I have been asked by auto mechanics when they have taken my keys while they fix my car and grocery store cashiers and children, "Why do you have a penny on your keychain?" I quickly tell them the story and say, "No matter how many mistakes I have made, or how scratched up I am by life, I can always remember that because of Jesus, I am worth full value."

When I came home from the retreat, our daughter Kacie was 9

years old and came home from school one day with tears in her eyes saying, "I'm not good enough and I don't matter." My heart broke. Then I was able to tell her about the woman in the Bible and how Jesus saw her, called her forward, touched her and healed her. And how he sees Kacie and she is worth full value because of Jesus.

She put the keychain on her backpack, and the message began to sink in. It is an important and true message. It is one worth sharing with everyone you meet.

> *"Are not two sparrows sold for a penny? Yet*
> *not one of them will fall to the ground outside*
> *your Father's care. And even the very hairs of*
> *your head are all numbered. So don't be afraid;*
> *you are worth more than many sparrows."*

(Matthew 10:29-31 New International Version)

Your Turn

What in your life has bent you over? What lies have you been believing? Who in your life would benefit from being told, "You are worth full value"?

_____

_____

_____

_____

_____

_____

_____

_____

_____

_____

_____

_____

_____

CHAPTER 20

Appreciate Differences

You've heard it said before, "opposites attract." Well, I have to agree. Although my husband and I have many interests in common and the most important matters of faith in common, in other ways we are very different. I tend to be more of an extrovert, and he tends to be more of an introvert. I tend to be glass half full, and he tends to be glass half empty. I would rather be on water, he would rather stay on land. He can focus while music is on, I prefer quiet. He tends to think about what is coming in the future; I am more in the present.

According to the Enneagram, a personality assessment, he is a Type 4 and I am a Type 7. He acts a bit like Eeyore and I act like Tigger.

I have grown in my understanding of how God has wired us both and have learned to appreciate our differences, instead of trying to change him. I have discovered that my personality of being positive and spontaneous and wanting everyone to be happy can at times take away from what others are experiencing. Kind of like when Tigger bounces through Rabbit's garden and makes a mess of everything.

I have begun to realize that when someone is not ok, it is ok, and I have been challenged to not rush through my own sad or negative emotions. It is ok for me to not always be bouncy and full of fun, fun, fun.

Every personality type has strengths and weaknesses. There is not one type that is better than another. We all have areas of growth and aspects of our personalities we can be stretched in. My Type 4 husband is creative, thoughtful, and able to express what he is feeling and thinking. I am thankful for who he is and how God has made him. I don't need Jeffrey to be more like me, because then he can't be himself. And I don't need to be more like him, because then I wouldn't be me.

"For we are God's masterpiece. He has created us anew in Christ Jesus, so we can do the good things he planned for us long ago."

(Ephesians 2:10 New Living Translation)

Your Turn

How well do you know yourself? What best recharges you? How do you react when you are stressed? What can you do to know yourself better? How can you appreciate the differences in those around you?

_____

_____

_____

_____

_____

_____

_____

_____

_____

_____

_____

_____

_____

_____

_____

_____

CHAPTER 21

Think Out Of The Box

It was August, and our youngest daughter, Alli, came to me and said, "I'm not going back to high school. I can't." And then she showed me her phone and what she had researched as another option for school and said, "Can I do this?" She had researched online schooling and wanted to know if she could complete her last two years of high school from home on the computer. I said, "Let's look into it, and see if we can make it happen."

School was never Alli's thing. She had several different learning challenges through the years and had worked hard at overcoming them. She attended her first two years of high school with her older sister, Abbey. When Abbey graduated and Alli realized she would be going there day after day alone, she stood up for what she needed and let us know the anxiety and stress was too much and that she wanted to find another way.

I wanted more than anything to find a way for this to work for her. I wanted her to succeed and not be miserable every day. I had no idea how to make this work and had never experienced this before.

Her three older sisters went to traditional brick and mortar schools. I was out of my comfort zone. I give her so much credit for researching another way on her own and admitting she needed and wanted something different. And I am so glad I listened to her.

For so many years I would cheerlead her out the front door, "You can do it!", "It's not so bad.", "Hang in there!". It was time to really listen to what she was feeling and try and make this happen. Remember, it was August, we had already missed the deadlines for enrollment into the virtual academy. We pursued it anyway.

She was accepted into the program, and we began to learn how this whole thing worked. It was like drinking from a firehose. So much information and everything was new to both of us.

What I saw happen over the next two years was nothing short of a miracle.

I watched our daughter go from dreading school to being motivated and an incredible self-starter. I used to have to talk her into going to school. Her last two years of high school I never once had to remind her to do her homework or listen to a class lecture. She took care of all the details. She put forth her best effort and did very well. We were so very proud of her. She was determined and didn't let any obstacle get in her way.

God taught me to trust him over and over again as Alli made her way toward graduation. God's got her! And I watched her faith and trust in God grow as well. We were so grateful for an alternative way to complete school. This online method worked great for her. She graduated from Wisconsin Virtual Academy and we had an awesome celebration with family and friends!

"For I can do everything through
Christ, who gives me strength."

(Philippians 4:13 New Living Translation)

Your Turn

Where have you needed to think outside the box? What are you hesitant to try because you've never done it that way before? What story from your life has helped you trust God more?

CHAPTER 22

T. J. A.

I'm a terrible back seat driver. Just ask my husband or any of my kids. I'm the one who gives the audible gasp if I think we are getting too close to the car in front of us. I use my foot on the imaginary break and hold on tightly to the door handle.

Except for when I am in Ethiopia.

Now, this makes no logical sense. The driving in Ethiopia is way more nerve-wracking and much more crowded, and there are way more obstacles (like donkeys and cows and bikes and people and motorcycles). And yet, I have a crazy amount of peace. I just ride along in the van and completely trust the driver.

I started to wonder why I was so different from one place to another. What was different about my mindset?

The first time I went to Ethiopia I learned this phrase, "T.I.A. — This is Africa". It is a way to say, "Expect the unexpected". Expect the power to go out; it eventually will come back on. Expect long delays as you enter the country to get your visa. Or sometimes you sail right through.

Each time I have gone to Ethiopia, I have had the privilege of being on an excellent team. The details are handled for me, and we always have a skilled driver that picks us up at the airport and takes us where we need to go. My mindset is one of trusting God for whatever may happen. I am purposeful about praying for each day without any other distractions of daily living back at home. I am focused on my purpose for being there, and God provides me with his perfect peace as I keep my mind and thoughts fixed on him. (Isaiah 26:3)

What would it look like if I treated every day like I was on a mission trip? Because that is really what life is: Each day covered in prayer, walking hand-in-hand with Jesus, asking him what He would like me to do and where I can be used by him, trusting He is in control and I am not.

I am not in control when I am in Ethiopia, and I am not in control when I am home. And I sure am thankful that God is.

"You will keep in perfect peace all who trust in you, all whose thoughts are fixed on you!"

(Isaiah 26:3 New Living Translation)

Your Turn

What might change if you awoke each day with the attitude: "I can't wait to see what God is going to do today!"? Think of a time in your life when you were intentional about fixing your thoughts on God and His presence. What was different for you?

_____

_____

_____

_____

_____

_____

_____

_____

_____

_____

_____

_____

_____

_____

_____

CHAPTER 23

Lauren Elizabeth

In 2014, my niece Lauren was diagnosed with leukemia. She was 27 years old and had just begun her career as a physical therapist. None of us could believe it.

She began her battle against this disease and fought with all her strength and determination. Her boyfriend, Trevor,  was by her side — and, in fact, they got married while she was at Duke hospital. They found her perfect bone marrow match and she was in full remission. We were all so thankful to God for the healing and the extra time with Lauren.

In 2017, the cancer returned. Lauren, once again, was brave and strong and prepared for battle. We had a family reunion in July of 2017 to celebrate my parents 60th wedding anniversary, and Lauren and Trevor were there. We laughed and enjoyed each other's company and celebrated love and family and the good gifts God has showered on each of us.

We all went back to our homes, and Lauren went back to fighting. The treatments they were trying were not working, and they began some experimental trials. While it began to work, her other organs could not handle what was being done to her. We were all shocked on the day we learned that God had called her home.

It was January 10, 2018. I was shopping at Target, and my sister called. I answered, and all I could hear was her sobbing and the words, "She's dead." I literally fell to the floor and began to weep with my sister. A stranger stopped to ask if I was okay, and I said, "No!"

I managed to pick myself up off the floor and made my way to a bench. My sister was calling me from a dentist parking lot in Tennessee. I made her promise me that she would wait until my parents or brother could get to her. I made the call to my brother and got his voicemail and then to my parents. They headed out to go and get my sister, and I called her back to wait on the phone with her.

There were no words in the moment that could be said. I just didn't want her to wait alone, and it was the only thing I could do from a distance.

In the days that followed, we had many more phone calls. And many more tears. We began to plan a family get-together to celebrate Lauren's life and to share the promises of God and the hope we have in Him with one another. The plans came together, and we gathered at my brother Scott's house in Indiana on February 10th.

My sister called to share with me what could be called a God Moment. She was paging through a hymnal at my brother's house and came across "The Old Rugged Cross". The chorus goes like this:

> So I'll cherish the old rugged Cross
> Till my trophies at last I lay down
> I will cling to the old rugged Cross
> And exchange it someday for a crown

She then sent me a picture of her dentist appointment reminder card from January 10th: It said, "Crown Delivery". And then we realized one more reminder — Revelation 2:10 (the date we were gathered 2/10), says this: "Be faithful unto death, and I will give you the **crown of life.**"

Yes, indeed, my sweet niece had received her crown and was dancing in heaven with her Savior Jesus. We miss her still. Our hearts still ache. We give thanks for the 30 years we had to know her and the amazing ways she blessed others while she was on this earth. We give thanks for the truth that Jesus is the resurrection and the life, and we will see her again.

> *"Jesus told her, "I am the resurrection and the life.*
> *Anyone who believes in me will live, even after dying."*

(John 11:25 New Living Translation)

Your Turn

Have you lost someone special? Write about the experience. In what ways does God comfort you and bring you hope? What have you learned about how to comfort others?

CHAPTER 24

Come And See, Stay And Listen, Go And Tell

After each one of our daughters were born, I wrote a little song to sing them. The "songs" are more like little ditties — just a few lines with an occasional rhyme. There have been other times when God has given me words and a little tune, usually inspired by the ocean or the mountains. They are just between me and Him, not for anyone else except maybe my family and they will certainly never show up on any kind of a CD.

I don't claim to be a songwriter. However, I am a speaker. I have enjoyed speaking at my church for a women's event called Advent By Candlelight for over 20 years. The evening consists of some special music, a devotional talk, dessert and conversation and the Christmas Gospel.

Several years ago, I was working on my talk and found myself landing on this topic; "Come and See, Stay and Listen, Go and Tell." I was driving to pick my kids up from school and started to sing some different rhyming lines. Before I knew it, I had a little song. I thought, "Wouldn't it be fun if my song could be sung at the event?" I recorded myself singing it and gave it to a talented friend who figured out the chords. And she sang it!

It was like a little dream come true for me. One of my "songs", which aren't usually heard outside of my home or my van, was sung for about 400 women.

Come and See the newborn King, listen to the
angels sing
Stay awhile by his side, in his love you can abide
Now Go and Tell the wondrous things you've
heard and seen
So that all will know, the joy and peace our
blessed Savior brings, the joy and peace our
blessed Savior brings.
Come Lord Jesus we need you, be the one that
we turn to
In your presence help us stay, Listen Jesus as we
pray
Now Go and Tell the wondrous things you've
seen and heard
So that all will know, the joy and peace our
blessed Savior brings, the joy and peace our
blessed Savior brings.

My "little" dream come true took some courage on my part to risk sharing it with my friend and asking her to sing it. She could have said "no" or, "It isn't good enough". Often when we have a dream there will be some risk involved. But there may be a greater risk if we don't pursue it and try and make it happen.

"Come and see what our God has done, what
awesome miracles he performs for people!"

(Psalm 66:5 New Living Translation)

Your Turn

What is something you dream of, big or small? Write out the details of your dream. What would it take to get you to pursue it? What is one small step you can take towards making it a reality?

CHAPTER 25

Ameseginalew

I never thought I would be able to say that I have been to Ethiopia seven times.

I have been blessed to be a part of the teaching team through the Pastoral Leadership Institute International. We help to train pastors and their wives in leadership and discipleship skills. It is a unique experience because the wives are included in the training as full participants. Some of the training sessions are done together, and some are separate for the men and women. I was privileged to lead the training with the women.

God taught me so many lessons over the years that I was blessed to go and be with my Ethiopian brothers and sisters in Christ. Here are a few of the lessons and observations from my time there.

- Although we have different cultures, we have more in common than I ever thought.

- Laughter and tears need no translation.

- The Ethiopian women pray with more passion than I have ever seen!

- They bring Romans 12:15 to life: "Rejoice with those who rejoice; mourn with those who mourn."

- Miracles and answered prayers happen!

- You don't have to teach Ethiopians how to practice hospitality or "neighboring". If you ever have experienced a coffee ceremony you will understand this.

- Not being in a hurry is a good thing.

- Saying thank you in the local language means a great deal to those who hear it—"ameseginalew."

- The standard greeting of a cheek to cheek kiss is warm and welcoming.

- Schedules for teaching are not nearly as important as stopping for buna (coffee) and time for fellowship.

- They know the meaning of their names and the stories that go with them.

- I know very little of sacrifice, risk or perseverance.

- I am comforted to remember that God is close to the broken hearted (Psalm 34:18).

- I always went home better than when I came — humbled, encouraged, inspired, thankful that one day we will spend eternity together.

> *"May the Lord keep watch between you and me when we are away from each other."*
>
> (Genesis 31:49 New International Version)

Your Turn

What have you learned or discovered from someone who is different than you? What did you learn about yourself? How did that experience change you?

Words Of Affirmation

For several years my husband, Jeff, gave a very meaningful gift to each of us girls (me and our 4 daughters) for Christmas. He would write us a letter full of words of affirmation. expressing his love for us. As we read his letters, tears would stream down our cheeks as our hearts filled, realizing how much he loves us.

One year, we decided we would each write a letter to on another. So instead of one letter, we had five. It was one of the most memorable Christmases we had, and there was an abundance of tears. Spoken words of affirmation are awesome. But words that are written down can be read over and over again, and the blessing continues to build you up and fill you with love.

For my mom's 80th birthday, my siblings and I had an idea. We each wrote 20 different things that we love about our mama and mailed them to her for her birthday. She absolutely loved it! She put them in a photo album and can continue to look at them again and again.

When my husband celebrated 25 years in ministry, I gathered as many notes of appreciation as I could from the many people whose lives he has touched from his ministry as a pastor. That notebook full of cards, notes, stories and memories is now a treasured possession and continues to encourage him.

For my birthday, my daughter made me a poster with all sorts of notes written about why she loves me. And her children told her what they wanted her to write. My 6-year-old granddaughter, Bailey, said, "She's the best Mimi in the world and I could never ask for a better one if I searched anywhere." And 2-year-old Emmey said, "because I just love her so much" repeated over and over again. WOW! Talk about feeling loved!

Words can make a powerful difference. I am sure we could all benefit if we shared words of affirmation and encouragement more often.

"Death and life are in the power of the tongue."

(Proverbs 18:21a English Standard Version)

Your Turn

When was the last time you wrote a love note? Who in your life needs to know how much they are loved? How could you use writing to fill them up with love?

_____

_____

_____

_____

_____

_____

_____

_____

_____

_____

_____

_____

_____

_____

_____

CHAPTER 27

Family And The Farm

Growing up, our family's Sunday rhythm always went like this: Church and Sunday School, before heading across the Mississippi River from St. Louis, MO, to Collinsville, IL, to visit my grandparents on their farm.

I cherish the many memories we made there: Walking hand-in-hand with my grandfather through the fields. Picking up the potatoes he would dig up. Eating more strawberries and raspberries and black raspberries than ever went into the bucket. Hunting for morel mushrooms. (I figured out very quickly to just follow Grandpa and look at the end of his shoe, it would be pointing right at the hidden mushroom). Ice skating on the frozen pond and warming up by the fire. Watching as the cousins and aunts and uncles gathered around after we picked apples, making apple cider. Reading under the big tree on one of the quilts that Grandma Rosie made. Swinging and climbing into the tree house. Learning the hard way about not going into the burn needles. Playing canasta and Kings Corners with Grandma. Setting the table for dinner (my job was to put out the napkins) and always saying a prayer before dinner and reading a devotion and giving thanks after. Planting a black walnut tree with Grandpa and being able to watch it grow over time. Eating the best fried chicken ever and fresh bread from the bakery. Playing in the truck full of soybeans. Giving thanks for the miracle that, when the barn collapsed on Grandpa, the beams provided a triangle over him and his life was spared.

I learned a lot about faith and love at my grandparents' farm. Easter egg hunts at first for family and then for kids from the church. The Christmas tree dripping with tinsel. Grandpa making the Christmas tree into a cross for Good Friday at the church and then celebrating that He is Risen on Easter. Feeling so loved as he showed me a special apple that he put  tape on in the shape of my initials and, when it ripened, he peeled off the tape, he handed me my very own personalized apple. After Grandma died, he took up baking and sent me chocolate chip cookies to college. He put a note in with the cookies that said, "Look, Min, no raisins."

Grandpa is the one who taught me about tithing. My first job was selling tomatoes. Grandpa let us take tomatoes home, and he would tell us what a fair price per pound would be to sell them. The only stipulation on what we did with the money we earned was to give the first 10 percent to church. We were taught to tithe. The gifts we were given came from God, and so we say thank you and give a portion back.

I can picture the red wagon that we pulled down White Avenue, the yellow scale we used to weigh the tomatoes, and the brown paper bags in which we placed the tomatoes that we sold to neighbors. I can remember the joy I had to be able to put some of the money we collected in the offering plate on Sunday.

Everything we have is a gift from God. None of it is ours. And all he asks is for a portion back to honor and thank him. What a wonderful lesson my Grandfather helped to teach us kids.

How grateful I am for my parents making it a priority to go each week to the farm. How blessed I am for having had a relationship with my grandparents and for the legacy of faith in Jesus.

> *"Every good and perfect gift is from above,*
> *coming down from the Father of the heavenly lights,*
> *who does not change like shifting shadows."*

(James 1:17 New International Version)

Your Turn

Reflect on the memories you have of your grandparents. What stories can you write down. Are you a grandparent now? What memories are you creating? What legacy do you want to pass on to the next generation through your children, family or the community?

_____

_____

_____

_____

_____

_____

_____

_____

_____

_____

_____

_____

_____

CHAPTER 28

Connecting With My Creator

Colorado is a beautiful place to be no matter what the season is. I have enjoyed snow skiing in the winter and the spring and have also enjoyed vacationing there in the summer. The mountains are breathtaking, and perhaps my favorite is the cool, rushing mountain streams with the massive boulders and small rocks. The wildflowers are beautiful, and I love how the

aspen leaves shake and rattle in the breeze. One summer, when I was taking some time by myself sitting on a giant rock by a stream, I was overwhelmed that when I am out appreciating God's creation, there are a multitude of ways I am connected with my Creator and learn more about His character.

In Avon, Colorado, there is the Eagle River in the Avon Whitewater Park, a section perfect for those who love to kayak–for really talented kayakers. I stopped and read the sign explaining more about this river: "While a large amount of Colorado rivers are controlled by dams, the Eagle River is one of the few that is free-flowing. This means the water you see in the river at any given time during the year came from snowmelt from the mountains high above the valley floor." I paused and immediately thought of God's grace. His grace is free-flowing. It is not controlled by me, and I have done nothing to deserve it. The informative sign went on to explain different common river terms, they were not common to me. One of the terms was an Eddy: "An Eddy is a place in a river where the water is moving in a different direction or different speed than the main current. Eddies are made by rocks in the river, outcroppings along the side, behind logs, and also on the inside of bends. Eddies are places where kayakers can sit and stay relatively still instead of floating downstream. It is a popular resting spot for kayakers." I immediately thought of Sabbath rest. Our creator God, on the seventh day of creation, took time to rest. He gave us the commandment to honor the Sabbath and keep it holy. He knew we would need time to rest. I think the definition of the Eddy describes the importance of taking time for Sabbath rest. We need to be moving in a different direction and at a different speed than the main current. Our culture moves at one speed and we, just like those in the kayaks, need to take a rest and be relatively still so we don't get swept downstream.

When I sat on the large rock, I thought of the Lord being my rock. "The Lord who is my rock, my fortress and my deliverer; my God is my rock, in whom I take refuge, my shield and the horn of my salvation, my stronghold." Psalm 18:2 When I stopped to take a video of the quaking aspen leaves blowing in the breeze, I was reminded of Isaiah 55:12, "You will go out in joy and be led forth in peace; the mountains and hills will burst into song before you, and all the trees of the field will clap their hands."

Yes indeed, the trees were clapping and praising God. When the sunshine was dancing on the stream, I thought of how Jesus is the light of the world, and in John 1:5 it says, "The light shines in the darkness, and the darkness has not overcome it." I was caught up in worshipping my awesome Heavenly Father and was beyond thankful that he makes himself known in his creation.

Hillsong United has a song that describes exactly what I am referring to: "So Will I" (100 Billion X), words and music by Joel Houston, Benjamin Hastings and Michael Fatkin. Look it up and listen to it. Close your eyes and picture the stars and the planets, the ocean and the mountains. If they were made to worship, so will I.

"Against its will, all creation was subjected to
God's curse. But with eager hope, the creation looks
forward to the day when it will join God's children
in glorious freedom from death and decay."

(Romans 8:20-21 New Living Translation)

Your Turn

When and where have you experienced God through His creation?
What lessons about His character did you learn? Where is one of
your favorite places to be to feel close to God?

_____

_____

_____

_____

_____

_____

_____

_____

_____

_____

_____

_____

_____

_____

_____

_____

_____

CHAPTER 29

Friends

I met her in 2003, when she led a breakout session on coaching at a conference my husband Jeff and I attended. Soon after she began to coach Jeff, I was fortunate enough to be coached by her. A few years later, we contracted with her to help us create a coaching culture at our church. I began to work closely with her to help train several people to be coaches. Every time we interact, I am challenged, encouraged, and learn something new. I am so grateful to have her as a part of my life. Somewhere in there, we shifted from a professional relationship to where I now call her friend.

Friend: Now there is a word that has confusing meaning. Especially with the use on social media, a friend can be someone you barely even know. We toss the word around with little value attached to it. What does it mean anyway? Do you have to have known a person for a certain amount of time before they qualify as a friend? What makes a good friend?

The Bible has a lot to say about friends. There are 170 verses in the Bible that make reference to "friend." Here are a few:

*"One who has unreliable friends soon comes to ruin, but
there is a friend who sticks closer than a brother."*

(Proverbs 18:24 New International Version)

*"A friend loves at all times, and a brother
is born for a time of adversity."*

(Proverbs 17:17 New International Version)

*"The Lord would speak to Moses face to
face, as one speaks to a friend."*

(Exodus 33:11a New International Version)

There are some famous friendships in the Bible and the names are even listed, for example: Job and his three friends, Eliphaz, Bildad and Zophar. At first, they were the picture-perfect friends who went to be with Job after he suffered tremendous loss. Job 2:11 says, *"When Job's three friends, Eliphaz the Temanite, Bildad the Shuhite and Zophar the Naamathite, heard about all the troubles that had come upon him, they set out from their homes and met together by agreement to go and sympathize with him and comfort him."* If you keep reading the account, though, you discover that those same three friends quickly became the picture of how NOT to be a good friend. God calls them out in Job 42:7 because they did not speak the truth about God, and they turned against Job.

Then there is David and his friend Jonathan, and Daniel had some amazing friends who were willing to help him stand strong when they were taken captive in Babylon.

Paul talks about a man, Onesiphorus, who was called a refreshing friend. (2 Timothy 1). I want to be known as a refreshing friend. I want people to leave better after spending time with me.

The Bible talks about what can wreck friendship as well:

> *"A perverse person stirs up conflict, and*
> *a gossip separates close friends."*
> (Proverbs 16:28 New International Version)

> *"Whoever would foster love covers over an offense, but*
> *whoever repeats the matter separates close friends."*
> (Proverbs 17:9 New International Version)

> *"Even my close friend, someone I trusted, one*
> *who shared my bread, has turned against me."*
> (Psalm 41:9 New International Version)

The Gospel of Luke tells us in chapter 22 about how one of Jesus' followers, Judas, betrayed him.

Certainly, part of having friendships is the difficulty and hurt that comes when there is betrayal and when gossip stirs up trouble.

We have different friends at different times in our lives. We can't possibly stay connected in the same way with all of our friends. We grow older and move away and life happens, and we meet new people.

And yet, with intentionality, we can stay connected with regular scheduled times to talk and meeting face-to-face. Then there are those friendships where you haven't talked for years and, when you are together, it is like no time has passed and the friendship is strong and solid. What a blessing those relationships are!

That reminds me of my mom: She is 80 years old and has maintained her friendship with the little girl who lived across the street from her when she was a child. They have been friends since she was 5 — that is a 75-year-long friendship! What a rare treasure!

There comes a time in life when you need to take inventory of your friends, those you need to be around more and those you need to limit. You have choices you can make, and you can be intentional about what type of friend you are to others.

"I no longer call you servants, because a servant does not know his master's business. Instead, I have called you friends, for everything that I learned from my Father I have made known to you."

(John 15:15 New International Version)

Your Turn

Take time to reflect on the friendships you have had in your life. Who would you like to contact and reconnect with? Who could you reach out to and encourage? Who do you need to limit time with?

CHAPTER 30

Still Learning

My husband, Jeff, and I were attending a two-day intensive training focused on discovering more about our unique purpose, a personal vision journey. (lifeYounique.com)

One of the exercises, in Session 3, Journey 1, The Younique Experience, Younique, challenged us to think through our "life drifts", those times when we get off course and head down an unhelpful path. We looked at what Jesus went through in the desert with the temptations he faced. The temptations fall in three categories: Approval, Appetite and Ambition. We were challenged to look back over the chapters of our own lives and determine where we have been tempted with life drifts and what lies we were believing from the enemy.

One of those for me fell under approval, "I'll never be enough," specifically, the fear that I am not smart enough. In fact, there are many times I can hear myself say, "I'm so stupid," or "Well, that was a dumb idea."

We left the training for the evening and pulled into our hotel parking lot. It was late and I was tired and knew I wouldn't have any time to work on my computer that evening so I just left it in the car. The next morning, as we were getting ready for the day, our phone rang. It was the police, and they needed to talk to us. Our car had been broken into along with several others in the parking lot and, sure enough, they stole my computer bag. Unbelievable! The worst part was that my favorite Bible was in my computer bag, with all sorts of notes I had written in it over the years.

After the shock wore off, as I stood with the police officer and was looking at the shattered glass all over the back seat and the ground, I immediately thought how stupid I was to leave my computer in the car.

Of course, my husband reassured me it was ok, and not my fault. The hassle that followed was great: repair the window, replace the computer, etc. How quickly it all happened, from learning about and identifying the life drifts and the lies I believe to the incident that had me face-to-face with the lie once again.

It took great effort to replace that lie with the truth: I am loved no matter what. Because of Jesus, I am enough. Jesus resisted the temptation surrounding approval, and he became rejected so I can be accepted.

I would love to say, the lesson was learned that day and I have not had any other struggles with it. Not so. The list is long, like the time I left the garage door open in the winter and the pipe froze and broke. That was an expensive mistake. Or the time when I was leading a workshop and made copies for the participants but only copied one side instead of both sides and had to make the correction while they waited. Oh my ... can you imagine the self talk on that one?

I have learned over time to replace the lie, with the truth: I am not stupid. Sometimes I forget things or make mistakes. And, more importantly, there is nothing I can do that will make God love me more or make Him love me less. He Loves Me. He loves me, mistakes and all. He loves me perfectly and completely. I am his daughter.

"Satisfy us in the morning with your unfailing love, that we may sing for joy and be glad all our days."

(Psalm 90:14 New International Version)

Your Turn

What life drifts do you struggle with?
Approval: "I'll never be enough" (shame)
Appetite: "I'll never have enough" (fear)
Ambition: "I'll never accomplish enough" (guilt)
What lies do you tell yourself? How can you replace it with truth?

_____

_____

_____

_____

_____

_____

_____

_____

_____

_____

_____

_____

_____

_____

CHAPTER 31

Adventure

The youth director at our church, Emily, pulled me aside and said, "Your daughter Abbey needs adventure. You will need to find ways to provide that for her, or she may go off and find it in unhealthy ways." I wasn't exactly sure what she meant. Abbey was only in the seventh grade at the time, and she was more of a soft-spoken, reserved kid. I don't think I would have said then that she had a great

need for adventure. However, I trusted Emily. She has worked with a lot of different kids, and God has gifted her with wisdom and discernment. So, I listened. It has been amazing to see this truth play out in Abbey's life.

When Abbey graduated from high school, she did not want to go the traditional route of stepping right into college. She took a look at several different gap year options and discovered a program sponsored by Tentmakers. It was a Year on Mission to live a Life on Mission. She had 40 days of training in northern Minnesota at a camp called Wilderness North. In addition to the excellent skills-based training the participants received, they also lived alone in separate cabins. She learned the invaluable skill of solitude and sabbath rest. After the intense 40 days, for nine months she lived in a community and was connected with a local church, worked a part-time job and taught the skills she had learned to high school students. The year concluded with a month abroad in the Czech Republic living out the skills they learned.

What an awesome experience. What an adventure! She valued the experience so much she went on staff with Tentmakers and stepped into the role of recruiting others for the program as well as being a trainer.

Since that time, she has traveled to Uganda alone on a vision trip, and to Ethiopia with me twice. She worked a summer job at the Sperry Chalet in Glacier National Park. Unfortunately, that adventure ended early because of the wild fires. Her most-recent adventure took her to Jerusalem, where she lived for six months volunteering at the Caspari Center. She is an amazing young lady who has found her voice, grown in confidence and trusts God to lead her as she follows Him. I can only imagine what adventures lie ahead for her.

"They will be like a tree planted by the water that sends out its roots by the stream. It does not fear when heat comes, its leaves are always green. It has no worries in a year of drought and never fails to bear fruit.'

(Jeremiah 17:8 New International Version)

Your Turn

What adventures have you gone on and what did you learn? What adventure would you like to go on? Maybe an adventure for you is not about international travel but it is walking across the street and introducing yourself to a neighbor or praying out loud with someone or learning a new skill.

Final Thoughts

There seem to be all sorts of reasons why people start and then stop journaling. I suppose it is like any other habit. When it is practiced over time and becomes part of your daily rhythm, and you understand the benefit, you stick with it.

I am inconsistent with many different areas of my life and there are a lot of projects I start and don't finish. There is however one area I have been very consistent with over many, many years and that is journaling. My journaling changed from what I did during the day to writing out my prayers: praising God for who he is, confessing where I had fallen short, thanking Him for what He has done and then asking for what I need and praying for others. Most of the time, it is a combination of writing about something I learned while reading God's word, writing out a prayer, and what happened during the day.

Whether you picked up this book because you love journaling or because you wanted to give it a try, I hope you have discovered the incredible blessing and gift journaling can be. It allows you to slow down and helps you process what is going on in your mind and heart. It enhances your connection with your Creator. It can be a running record of what you are grateful for. When you occasionally read back over what you have written (I do this at the end of the year), you will be amazed at the faithfulness of God and see his fingerprints all over your story. You can see how he guided, directed, protected and provided for you and others.

Keep going! Keep writing God! Keep praising him for who he is and thanking him for what he has done. Keep up the rhythm of reflecting on what took place in your day and recording it. Keep sharing snapshots of your story with others so they can know how good God is and how much He loves them.

I would love to hear from you. Drop me an email at amycmeyer10@gmail.com and let me know what you began to discover as you journaled about your stories. You can visit my website at amymeyer.org. You can contact me to plan a journaling workshop or Connecting with Your Creator Retreat. If you would rather text or call you can reach me at 608.217.9967. May God bless you as He continues to write your story.

A few tips for journaling

1. If you don't have a lot of time, or you don't enjoy writing in paragraph style, try writing out bullet points. Short statements or separate thoughts. I sometimes do this when I travel and am exhausted yet want to remember what took place during the day.

2. A very helpful place to begin, especially if you are wanting to create a journaling habit is to write down three things you are thankful for at the end of every day. Write at the same time every day. Growing in expressing gratitude will increase your joy and your contentment.

3. Some people hesitate to journal because once they get started they can't stop. They enjoy it so much that it takes a significant chunk of time so when they don't have that much time they just don't journal. Try setting a timer and only let yourself write for 20 minutes. Or try writing 3 times a day for 10 minutes.

4. If you find that you are intimidated by too much blank space that you think you have to fill, try dividing up the page and allow yourself a few lines per day. One of my favorite resources is the Pray! Prayer Journal Daily steps toward praying God's heart by Dean Ridings. There is a small section for every day of the month with different themes and helpful prayer resources throughout the journal.

5. I have a friend who doesn't want to journal because she does not want anyone else to read it. It is ok to write and then put it through a shredder or throw it away. (you will

miss out on the blessing of looking back at it over time) I know of others who have told a trusted friend or child that upon their death they are to burn the journals.

6. Practice freedom. There are no rules you have to follow. It needs to work for you. If you don't like lines, then have a blank page. If you need structure then divide a journal into 4 parts, Adoration, Confession, Thanksgiving, Supplication. Experiment with a variety of ways to write down what you are feeling, thinking and learning.

Some questions to help you get started or to continue the practice of journaling:

- What made you laugh today?

- What makes you sad?

- What ticks you off?

- What makes your heart sing?

- What would you do if you weren't afraid?

- What is your dream job?

- Where did you see God at work today?

- What do you love about where you live?

- If you had a magic wand what would you change about your city?

- What was your favorite gift you received? What was your favorite gift you gave?

- Describe how you would spend 24 hours if you could do whatever you wanted.